Impressum
Verlag: BABADADA GmbH, Nedderfeld 112 , 22529 Hamburg
Geschäftsführer / Verlagsleitung: Harald Hof
Druck: Books on Demand GmbH, In de Tarpen 42, 22848 Norderstedt

Imprint
Publisher: BABADADA GmbH, Nedderfeld 112 , 22529 Hamburg, Germany
Managing Director / Publishing direction: Harald Hof
Print: Books on Demand GmbH, In de Tarpen 42, 22848 Norderstedt

school

school

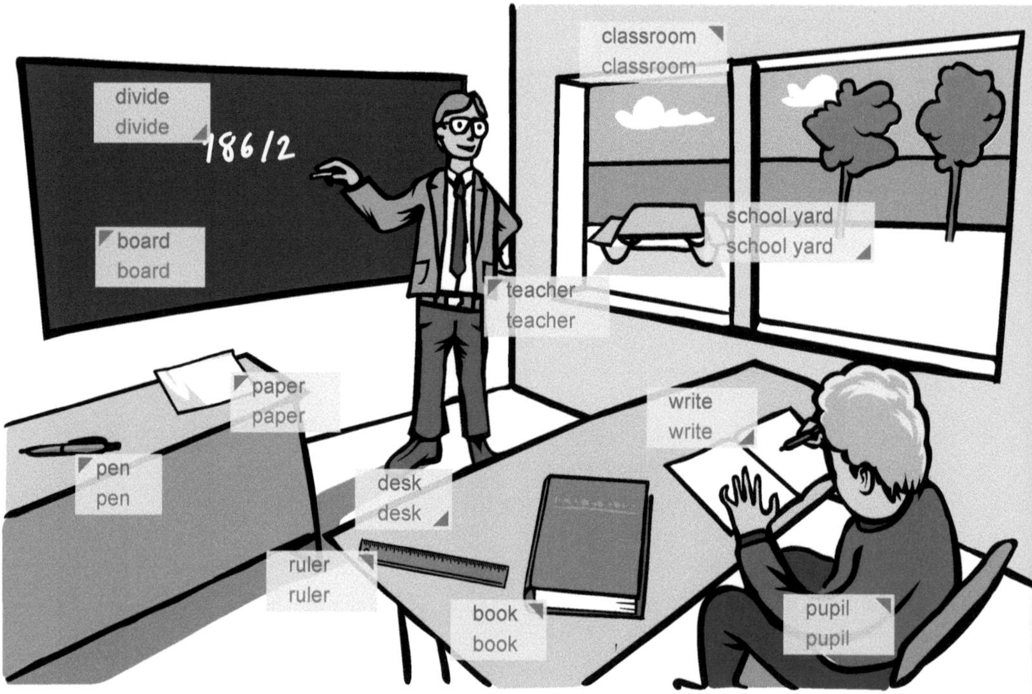
classroom
classroom
divide
divide
186/2
board
board
school yard
school yard
teacher
teacher
paper
paper
write
write
pen
pen
desk
desk
ruler
ruler
book
book
pupil
pupil

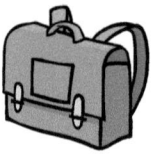

satchel

satchel

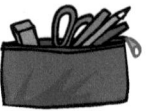

pencil case

pencil case

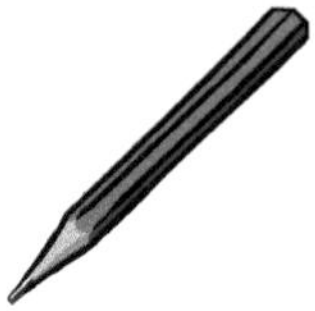

pencil

pencil

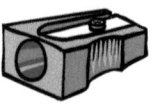

pencil sharpener

pencil sharpener

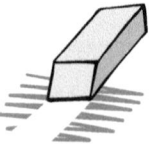

rubber

rubber

drawing pad

drawing pad

drawing

drawing

paintbrush

paintbrush

paint box

paint box

scissors

scissors

glue

glue

exercise book

exercise book

homework

homework

number

number

add

add

subtract

subtract

multiply

multiply

calculate

calculate

letter

letter

alphabet

alphabet

word

word

text

text

read

read

chalk

chalk

lesson

lesson

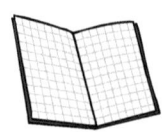

register

register

examination

exam

certificate

certificate

school uniform

school uniform

education

education

encyclopedia

encyclopedia

university

university

microscope

microscope

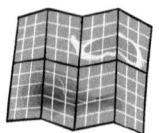

map

map

waste-paper basket

waste-paper basket

travel

travel

Grand
hotel
hotel
hostel
hostel
ROOMS
EXCHANGE
currency exchange office
bureau de change
car
car

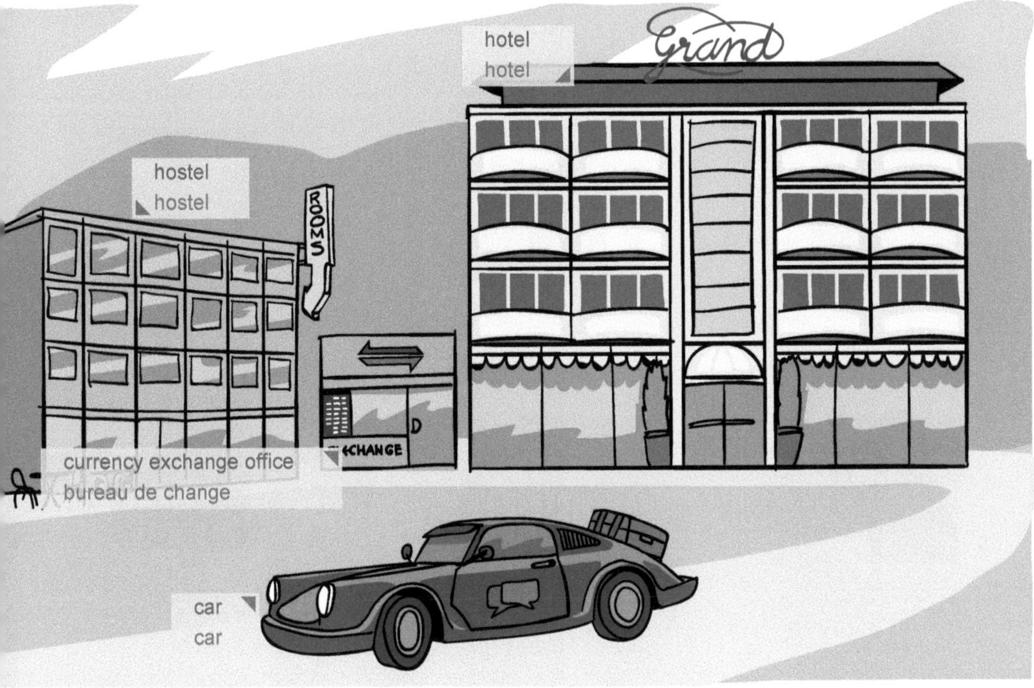

language

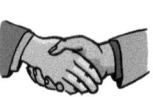

language

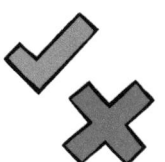

yes / no

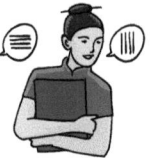

yes / no

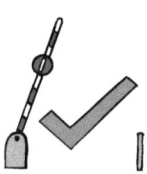

Okay

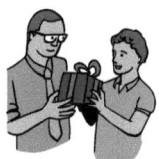

Okay

hello

hello

translator

translator

Thank you

Thank you

how much is...?

how much is...?

I don´t get it

I do not understand

problem

problem

Good evening!

Good evening!

Good morning!

Good morning!

Good night!

Good night!

goodbye

bye bye

direction

direction

luggage

luggage

bag

bag

backpack

backpack

guest

guest

room

room

sleeping bag

sleeping bag

tent

tent

tourist information

tourist information

beach

beach

credit card

credit card

breakfast

breakfast

lunch

lunch

dinner

dinner

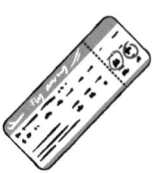

Ticket

ticket

elevator

lift

stamp

stamp

border

border

customs

customs

embassy

embassy

visa

visa

passport

passport

transport
transport

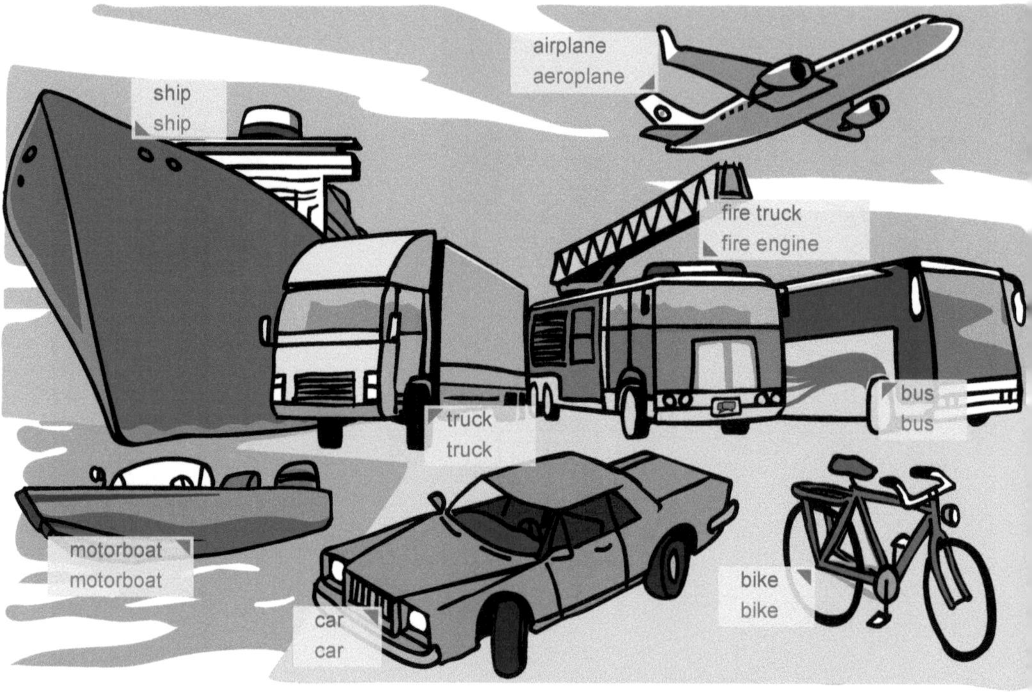

airplane
aeroplane
ship
ship
fire truck
fire engine
truck
truck
bus
bus
motorboat
motorboat
bike
bike
car
car

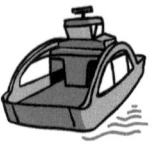

ferry

ferry

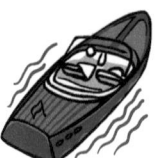

boat

boat

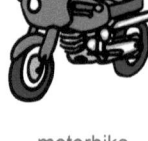

motorbike

motorbike

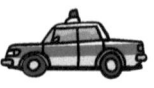

police car

police car

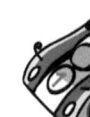

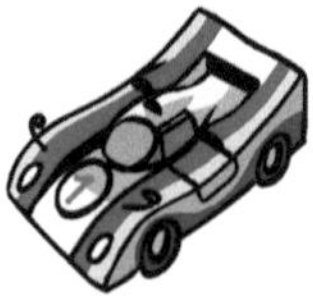

racing car

racing car

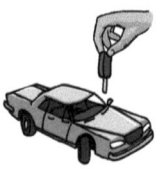

rental car

rental car

car sharing
car sharing

tow truck
breakdown truck

garbage truck
refuse truck

engine
motor

fuel
fuel

fuel station
petrol station

traffic sign
traffic sign

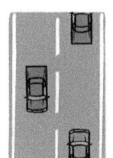

·traffic
traffic

traffic jam
traffic jam

parking lot
car park

train station
train station

tracks
tracks

train
train

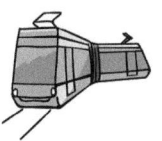

tram
tram

wagon
carriage

helicopter
helicopter

airport
airport

tower
tower

passenger
passenger

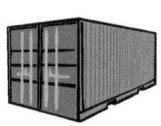

container
container

carton
carton

cart
cart

basket
basket

take off / land
take off / land

village
village

city center
city centre

house
house

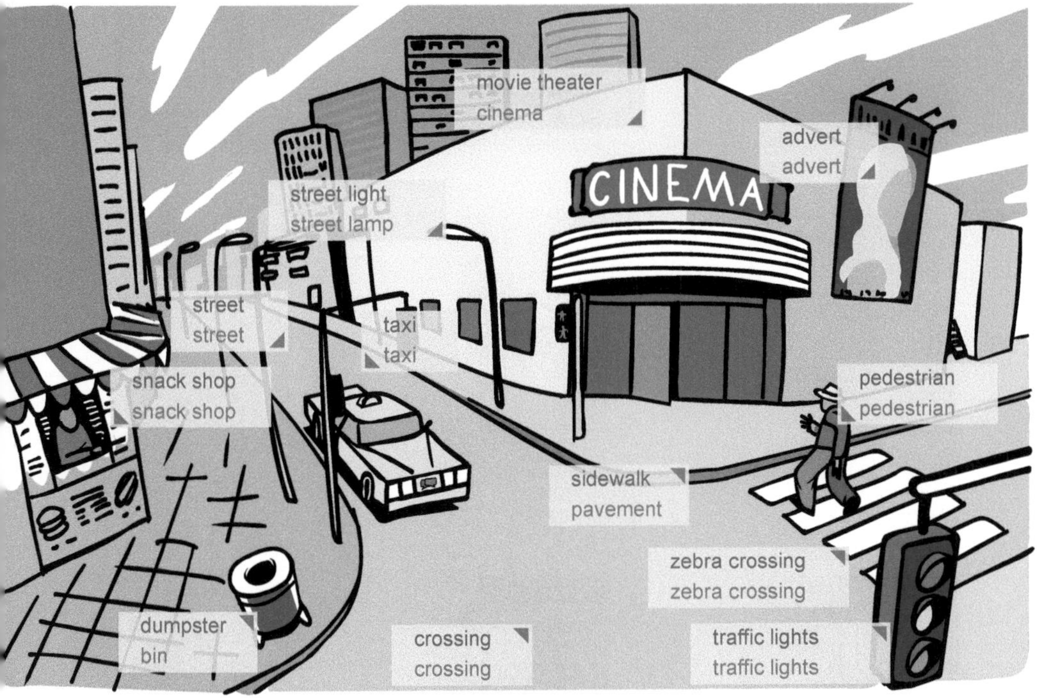

movie theater
cinema

advert
advert

street light
street lamp

CINEMA

street
street

taxi
taxi

pedestrian
pedestrian

snack shop
snack shop

sidewalk
pavement

zebra crossing
zebra crossing

dumpster
bin

crossing
crossing

traffic lights
traffic lights

hut
hut

apartment
flat

train station
train station

city hall
town hall

museum
museum

school
school

university

university

bank

bank

hospital

hospital

hotel

hotel

pharmacy

pharmacy

office

office

book shop

book shop

shop

shop

flower shop

florist's

supermarket

supermarket

market

market

department store

department store

fishmonger's shop

fishmonger's

mall

shopping centre

harbor

harbour

park
park

bench
bench

bridge
bridge

stairs
stairs

subway
underground

tunnel
tunnel

bus stop
bus stop

bar
bar

restaurant
restaurant

postbox
postbox

street sign
street sign

parking meter
parking meter

zoo
zoo

swimming pool
swimming pool

mosque
mosque

farm

farm

pollution

pollution

cemetery

graveyard

church

church

playground

playground

temple

temple

landscape

landscape

signpost
signpost

path
way

meadow
meadow

stone
stone

tree
tree

hiker
hiker

river
river

grass
grass

flower
flower

landscape - landscape

valley

valley

hill

hill

lake

lake

forest

forest

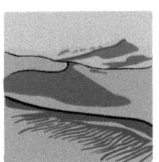
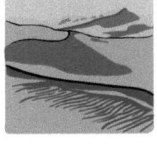

desert

desert

volcano

volcano

castle

castle

rainbow

rainbow

mushroom

mushroom

palm tree

palm tree

mosquito

mosquito

fly

fly

ant

ant

bee

bee

spider

spider

beetle

beetle

frog

frog

squirrel

squirrel

hedgehog

hedgehog

hare

hare

owl

owl

bird

bird

swan

swan

boar

boar

deer

deer

moose

moose

dam

dam

wind turbine

wind turbine

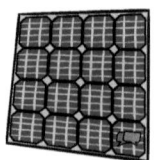

solar panel

solar panel

climate

climate

restaurant

restaurant

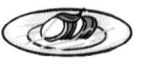

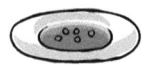

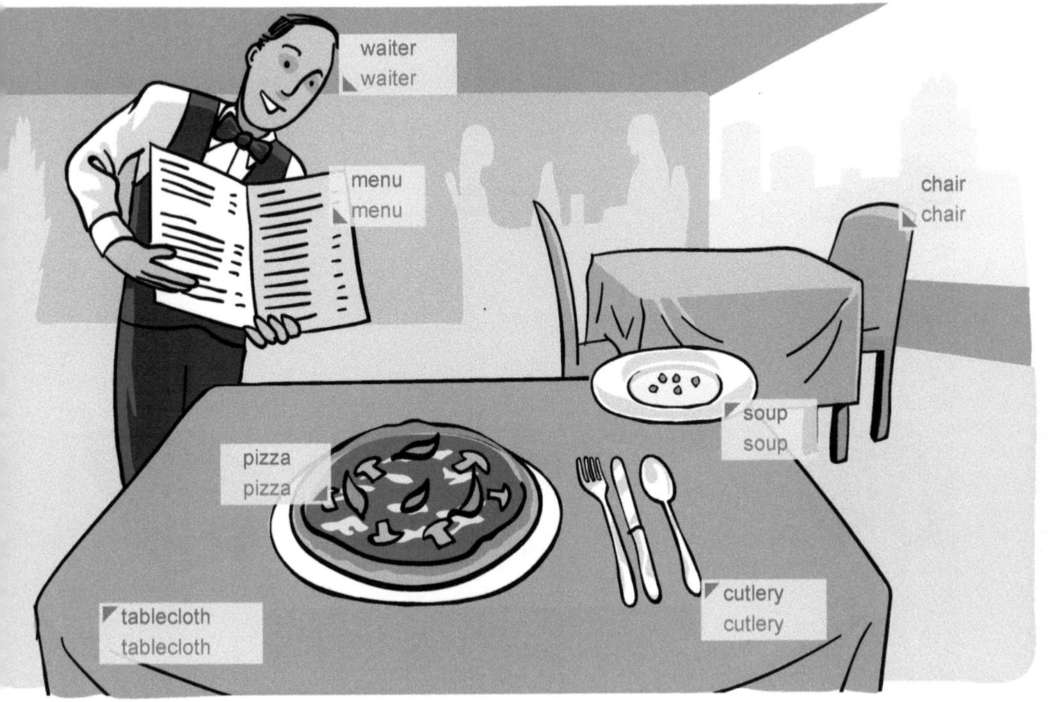
waiter
waiter
menu
menu
chair
chair
soup
soup
pizza
pizza
cutlery
cutlery
tablecloth
tablecloth

starter
starter

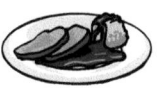

main course
main course

dessert
dessert

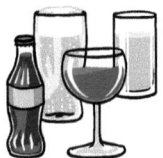

drinks
drinks

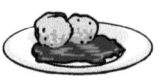

food
food

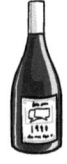

bottle
bottle

fast food

fast food

street food

street food

teapot

teapot

sugar bowl

sugar bowl

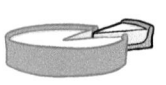

portion

portion

espresso machine

espresso machine

high chair

high chair

bill

bill

tray

tray

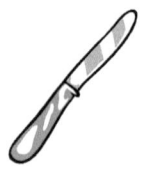

knife

knife

fork

fork

spoon

spoon

teaspoon

teaspoon

serviette

serviette

glass

glass

plate

plate

soup plate

soup plate

saucer

saucer

sauce

sauce

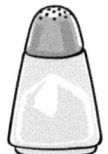

salt shaker

salt pot

pepper mill

pepper mill

vinegar

vinegar

oil

oil

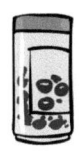

spices

spices

ketchup

ketchup

mustard

mustard

mayonnaise

mayonnaise

supermarket

supermarket

special offer
special offer
FOR
customer
customer
dairy products
dairy
fruit
fruit
shopping cart
trolley

BUTCHERS

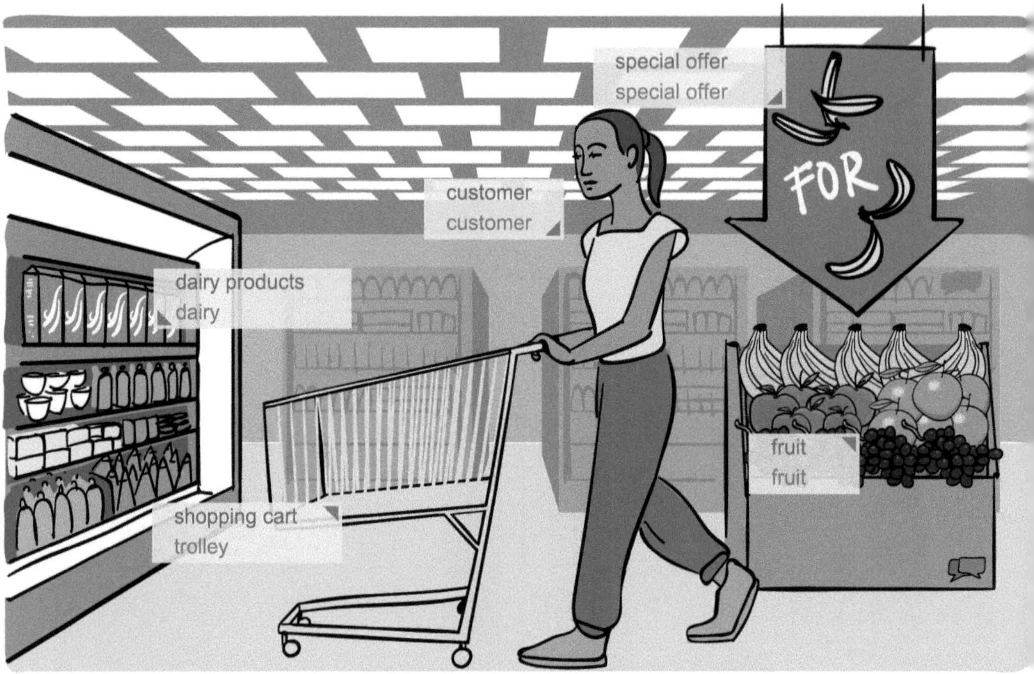

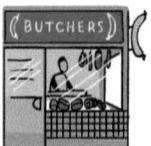

butcher's shop

butcher´s

BAKERY

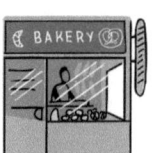

bakery

baker´s

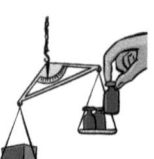

weigh

weigh

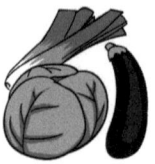

vegetables

vegetables

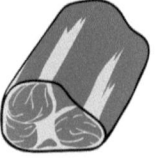

meat

meat

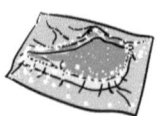

frozen food

frozen food

cold cuts

cold meat

canned food

tinned food

detergent

washing powder

candy

sweets

household products

household products

cleaning products

cleaning products

sales representative

salesperson

cash register

till

cashier

cashier

shopping list

shopping list

opening hours

opening hours

wallet

wallet

credit card

credit card

bag

bag

plastic bag

plastic bag

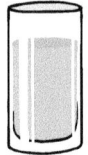

water

water

juice

juice

milk

milk

coke

coke

wine

wine

beer

beer

alcohol

alcohol

cocoa

cocoa

tea

tea

coffee

coffee

espresso

espresso

cappuccino

cappuccino

banana

banana

apple

apple

orange

orange

melon

melon

lemon

lemon

carrot

carrot

garlic

garlic

bamboo

bamboo

onion

onion

mushroom

mushroom

nuts

nuts

noodles

noodles

spaghetti

spaghetti

rice

rice

salad

salad

fries

chips

fried potatoes

fried potatoes

pizza

pizza

hamburger

hamburger

sandwich

sandwich

escalope

cutlet

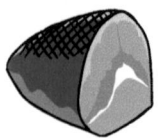

ham

ham

salami

salami

sausage

sausage

chicken

chicken

roast

roast

fish

fish

food - food

porridge oats

porridge oats

muesli

muesli

cornflakes

cornflakes

flour

flour

croissant

croissant

bread roll

bread roll

bread

bread

toast

toast

cookies

biscuits

butter

butter

curd

curd

cake

cake

egg

egg

fried egg

fried egg

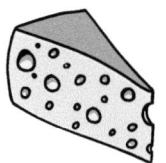

cheese

cheese

ice cream
ice cream

sugar
sugar

honey
honey

jelly
jam

nougat cream
chocolate spread

curry
curry

farm

farm

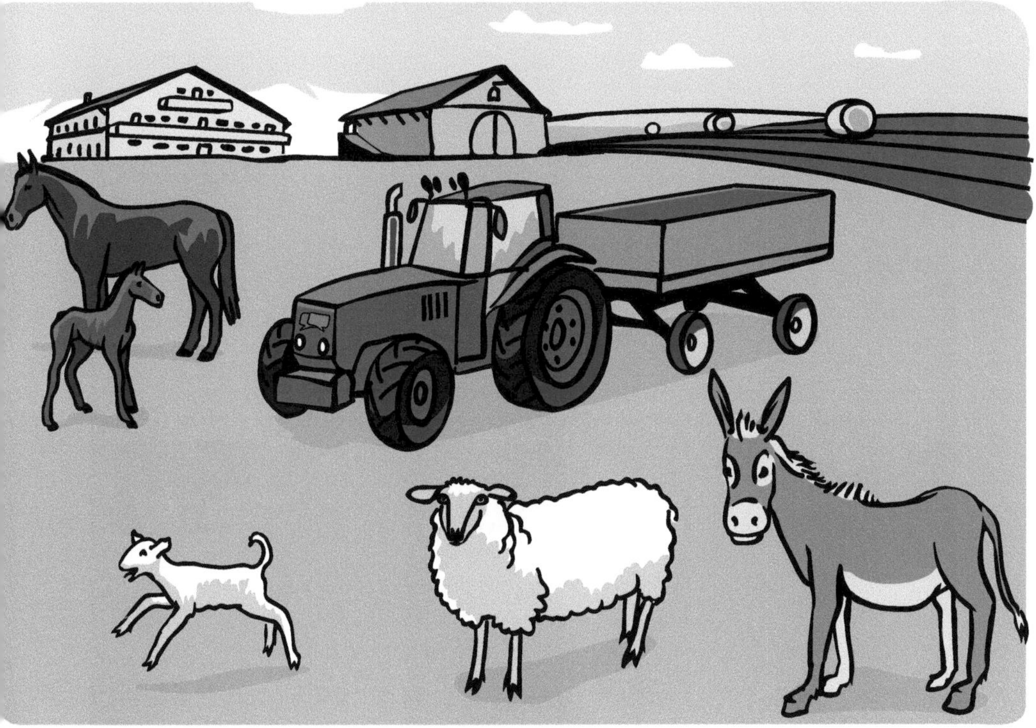

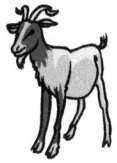

goat

goat

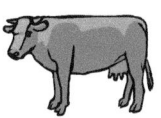

cow

cow

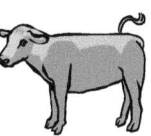

calf

calf

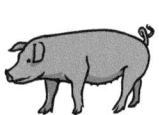

pig

pig

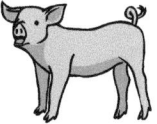

piglet

piglet

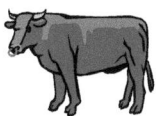

bull

bull

goose

goose

duck

duck

chick

chick

hen

hen

cockerel

cock

rat

rat

cat

cat

mouse

mouse

ox

ox

dog

dog

dog house

doghouse

garden hose

garden hose

watering can

watering can

scythe

scythe

plow

plough

sickle
sickle

hoe
hoe

pitchfork
pitchfork

axe
axe

pushcart
wheelbarrow

trough
trough

milk can
milk can

sack
sack

fence
fence

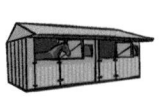

stable
stable

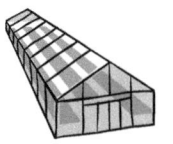

greenhouse
greenhouse

soil
soil

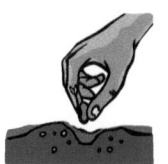

seed
seed

fertilizer
fertilizer

combine harvester
combine harvester

harvest

harvest

harvest

harvest

yams

yams

wheat

wheat

soya

soy

potato

potato

corn

corn

rapeseed

rapeseed

fruit tree

fruit tree

manioc

cassava

grain

cereals

house

house

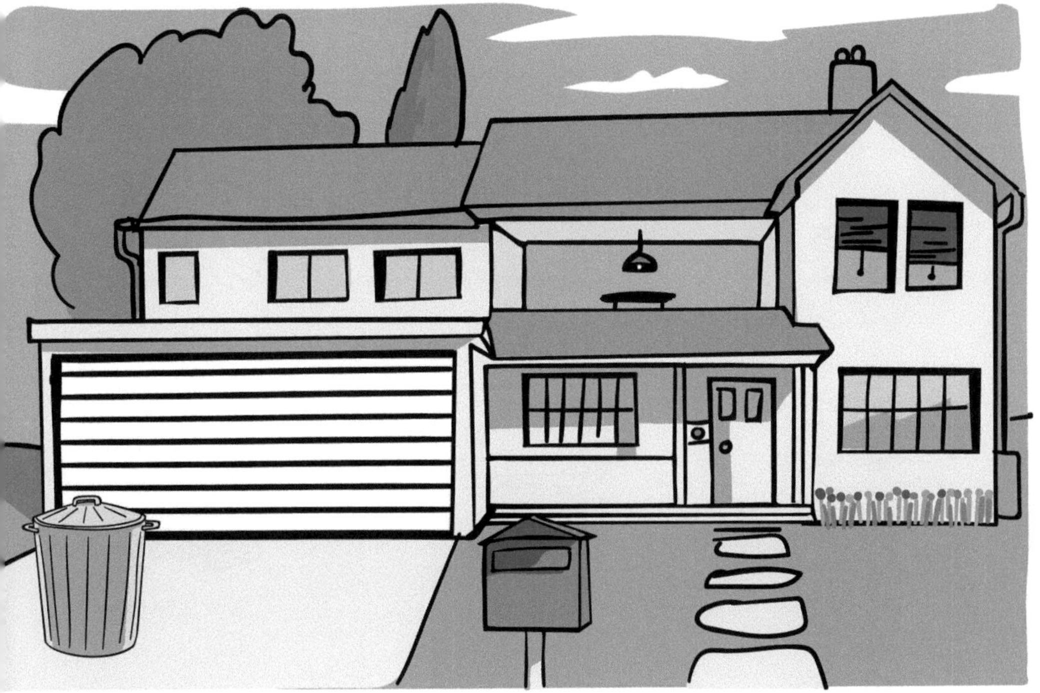

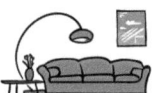

living room
....
living room

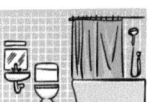

bathroom
....
bathroom

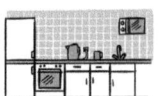

kitchen
....
kitchen

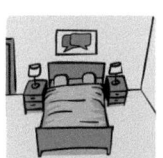

bedroom
....
bedroom

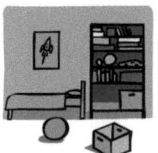

kids room
....
child's room

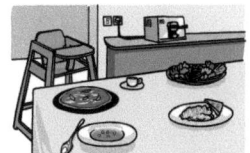

dining room
....
dining room

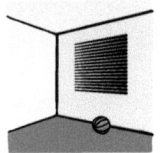

floor

floor

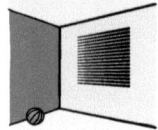

wall

wall

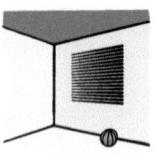

ceiling

ceiling

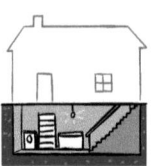

cellar

cellar

sauna

sauna

balcony

balcony

terrace

terrace

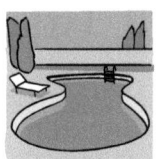

pool

pool

lawn mower

lawn mower

sheet

sheet

bedspread

bedspread

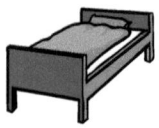

bed

bed

broom

broom

bucket

bucket

switch

switch

living room
living room

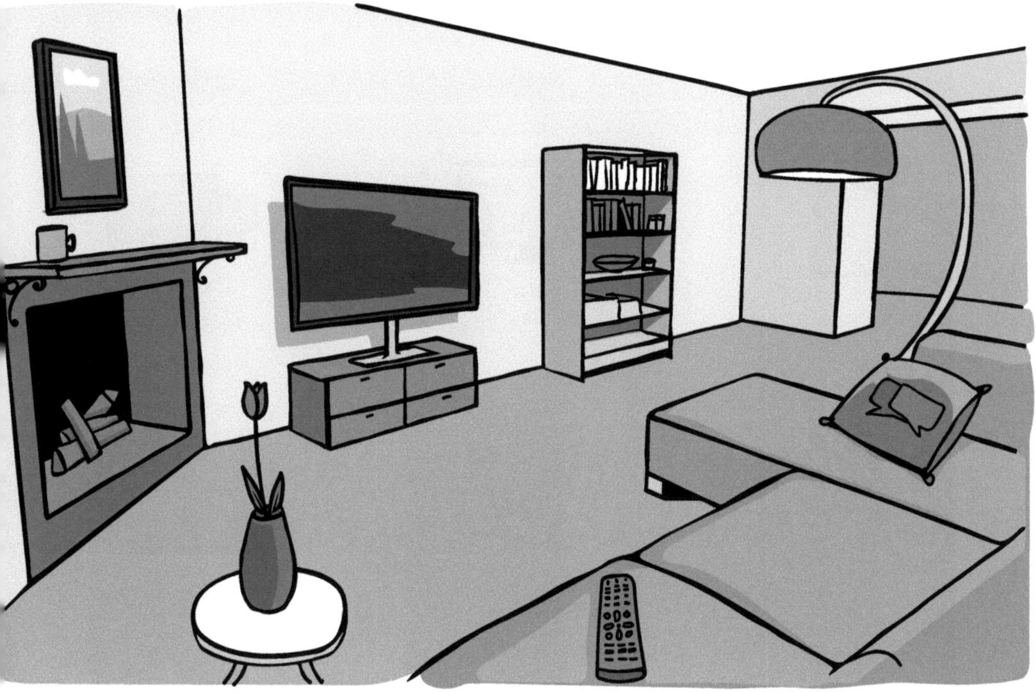

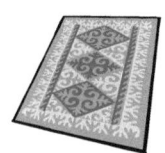

carpet

carpet

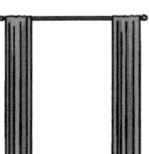

drape

curtain

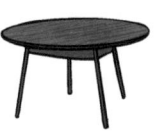

table

table

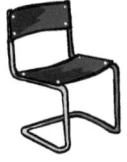

chair

chair

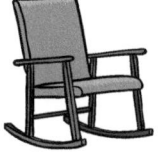

rocking chair

rocking chair

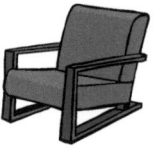

armchair

armchair

book
book

blanket
blanket

decoration
decoration

firewood
firewood

film
film

stereo system
hi-fi equipment

key
key

newspaper
newspaper

painting
painting

poster
poster

radio
radio

notebook
notepad

vacuum cleaner
hoover

cactus
cactus

candle
candle

kitchen
kitchen

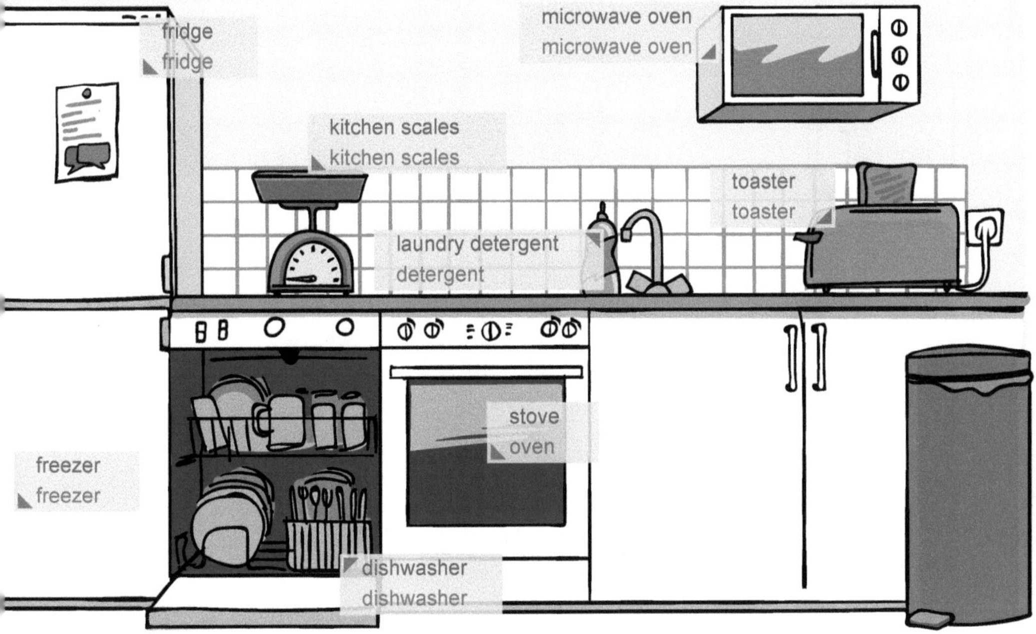
fridge
fridge
microwave oven
microwave oven
kitchen scales
kitchen scales
toaster
toaster
laundry detergent
detergent
stove
oven
freezer
freezer
dishwasher
dishwasher

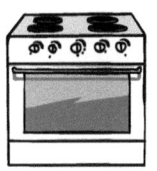

cooker
cooker

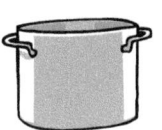

pot
pot

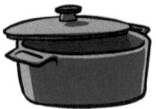

cast-iron pot
cast-iron pot

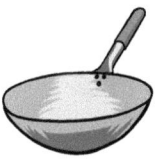

wok / kadai
wok / kadai

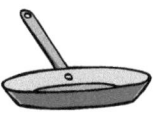

pan
pan

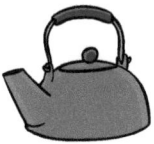

kettle
kettle

steamer

steamer

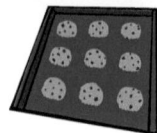

baking tray

baking tray

crockery

crockery

mug

mug

bowl

bowl

chopsticks

chopsticks

ladle

ladle

spatula

spatula

whisk

whisk

strainer

strainer

sieve

sieve

grater

grater

mortar

mortar

barbecue

barbecue

fireplace

open fire

chopping board

chopping board

rolling pin

rolling pin

corkscrew

corkscrew

can

can

can opener

can opener

oven cloth

pot holder

sink

sink

brush

brush

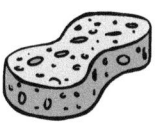

sponge

sponge

blender

blender

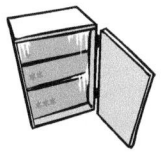

deep freezer

deep freezer

baby bottle

baby bottle

tap

tap

bathroom

bathroom

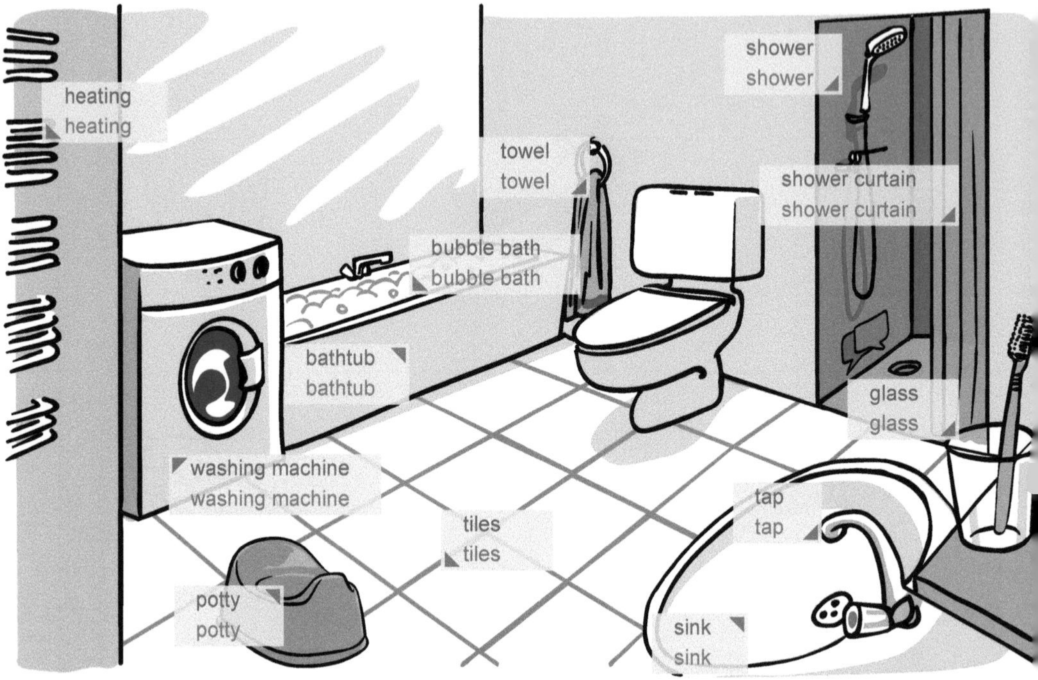
heating
heating
shower
shower
towel
towel
shower curtain
shower curtain
bubble bath
bubble bath
bathtub
bathtub
glass
glass
washing machine
washing machine
tap
tap
tiles
tiles
potty
potty
sink
sink

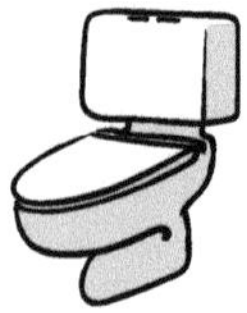

toilet

toilet

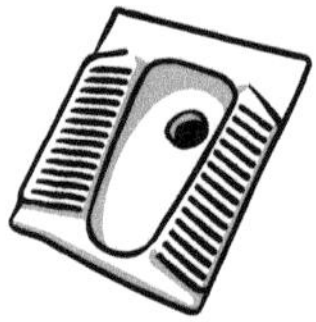

squat toilet

squat toilet

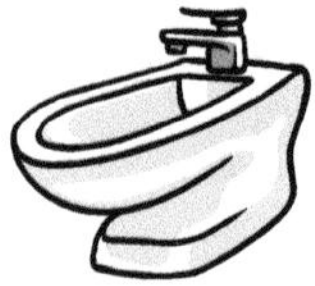

bidet

bidet

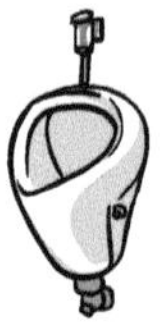

urinal

urinal

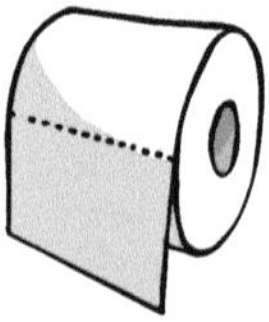

toilet paper

toilet paper

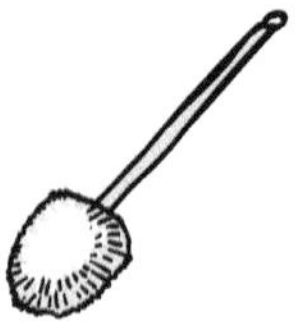

toilet brush

toilet brush

toothbrush

toothbrush

toothpaste

toothpaste

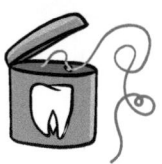

dental floss

dental floss

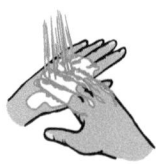

wash

wash

hand shower

handheld shower

douche

douche

basin

basin

back brush

back brush

soap

soap

shower gel

shower gel

shampoo

shampoo

flannel

flannel

drain

drain

creme

cream

deodorant

deodorant

mirror

mirror

hand mirror

hand mirror

razor

razor

shaving foam

shaving foam

aftershave

aftershave

comb

comb

brush

brush

hair-dryer

hair dryer

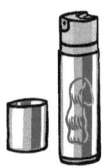

hairspray

hairspray

makeup

makeup

lipstick

lipstick

nail varnish

nail varnish

cotton wool

cotton wool

nail scissors

nail scissors

perfume

perfume

washbag
washbag

stool
stool

weighing scales
weighing scale

bathrobe
bathrobe

rubber gloves
rubber gloves

tampon
tampon

sanitary towel
sanitary towel

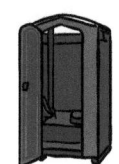

chemical toilet
chemical toilet

kids room

child's room

alarm clock
alarm clock
cuddly toy
cuddly toy
toy car
toy car
rattle
rattle
doll's house
doll's house
present
present

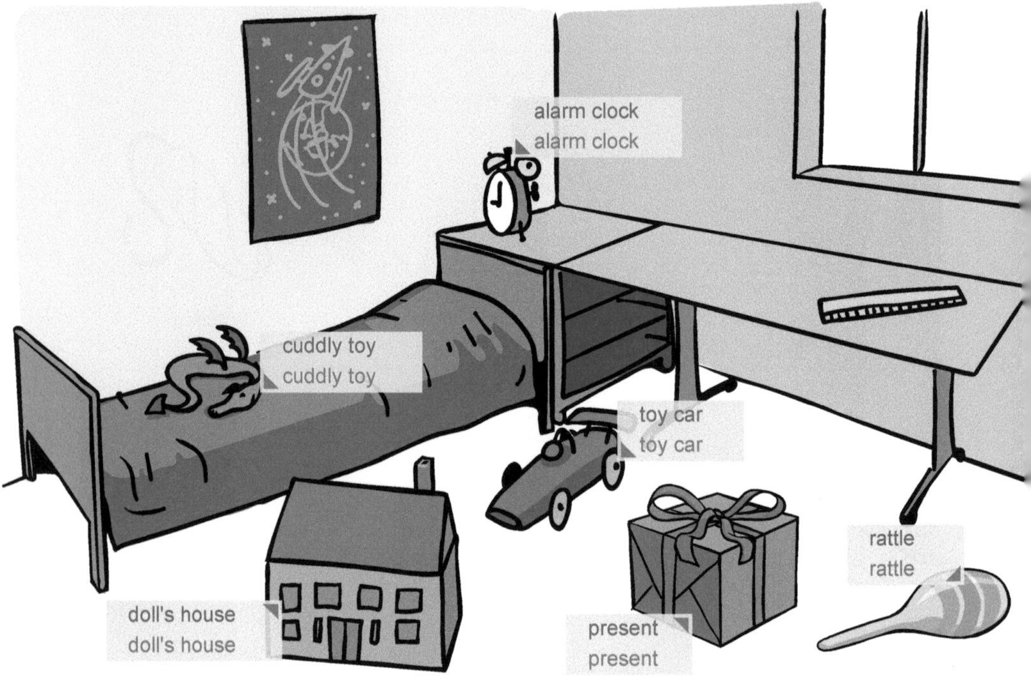

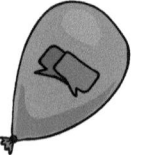

balloon

balloon

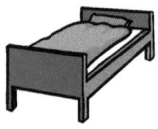

bed

bed

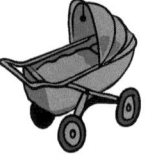

stroller

pram

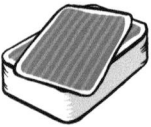

deck of cards

deck of cards

jigsaw

jigsaw

SUPER
MEGA

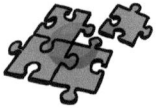

comic

comic

lego bricks

lego bricks

toy blocks

building blocks

action figure

action figure

romper suit

babygrow

frisbee

frisbee

mobile

mobile

board game

board game

dice

dice

model train set

model train set

pacifier

dummy

party

party

picture book

picture book

ball

ball

doll

doll

play

play

sandpit

sandpit

swing

swing

toys

toys

video game console

video game console

tricycle

tricycle

teddy bear

teddy bear

wardrobe

wardrobe

clothing

clothing

socks

socks

stockings

stockings

tights

tights

scarf
scarf

umbrella
umbrella

t-shirt
t-shirt

belt
belt

boots
boots

slippers
slippers

sneakers
trainers

sandals
sandals

shoes
shoes

rubber boots
rubber boots

underwear
underpants

bra
bra

undershirt
vest

body
body

pants
trousers

jeans
jeans

skirt
skirt

blouse
blouse

shirt
shirt

pullover
pullover

sweater
hoodie

blazer
blazer

jacket
jacket

coat
coat

raincoat
raincoat

costume
costume

dress
dress

wedding dress
wedding dress

suit
suit

nightgown
nightgown

pajamas
pyjamas

sari
sari

headscarf
headscarf

turban
turban

burka
burqa

kaftan
kaftan

abaya
abaya

swimsuit
swimsuit

trunks
trunks

shorts
shorts

tracksuit
tracksuit

apron
apron

gloves
gloves

button

button

glasses

glasses

bracelet

bracelet

necklace

necklace

ring

ring

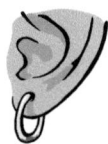

earring

earring

cap

cap

coat hanger

coat hanger

hat

hat

tie

tie

zip

zip

helmet

helmet

braces

braces

school uniform

school uniform

uniform

uniform

bib
bib

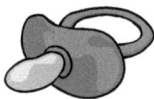

pacifier
dummy

diaper
nappy

office
office

server
server

filing cabinet
filing cabinet

printer
printer

paper
paper

monitor
monitor

mouse
mouse

desk
desk

folder
folder

keyboard
keyboard

chair
chair

waste-paper basket
waste-paper basket

computer
computer

coffee mug
coffee mug

calculator
calculator

internet
internet

laptop

laptop

letter

letter

message

message

cell phone

mobile

network

network

photocopier

photocopier

software

software

telephone

telephone

plug socket

plug socket

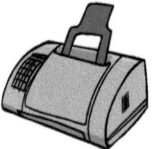

fax machine

fax machine

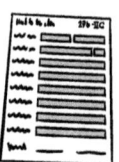

form

form

document

document

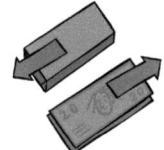

buy

buy

pay

pay

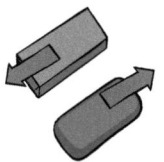

trade

trade

money

money

 **USD**

dollar

dollar

 **EUR**

euro

euro

 **JPY**

yen

yen

 **RUB**

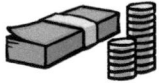

rouble

rouble

 **CHF**

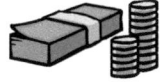

Swiss franc

Swiss franc

 **CNY**

renminbi yuan

renminbi yuan

 **INR**

rupee

rupee

cash point

cashpoint

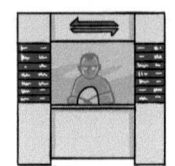

currency exchange office

bureau de change

gold

gold

silver

silver

oil

oil

energy

energy

price

price

contract

contract

tax

tax

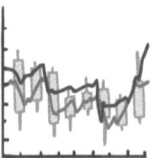

stock

stock

work

work

employee

employee

employer

employer

factory

factory

shop

shop

economy - economy

occupations
occupations

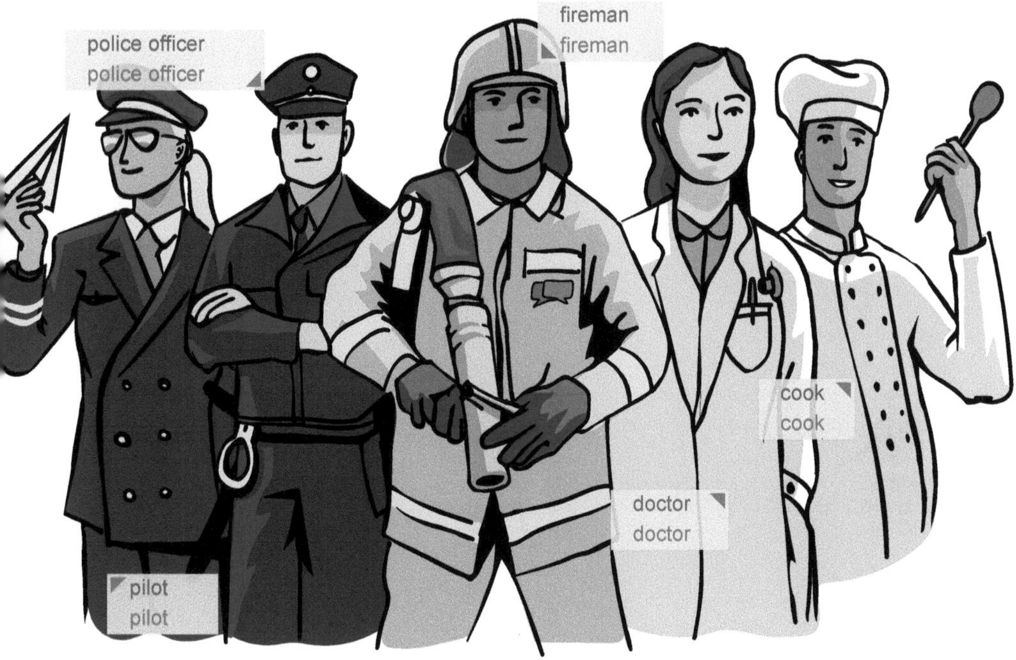
police officer
police officer
fireman
fireman
cook
cook
doctor
doctor
pilot
pilot

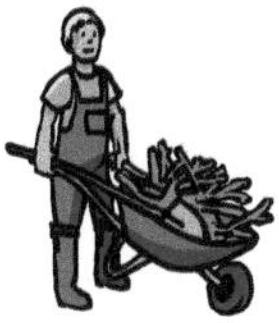

gardener

gardener

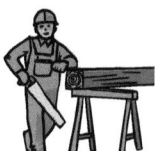

carpenter

carpenter

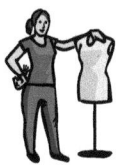

seamstress

seamstress

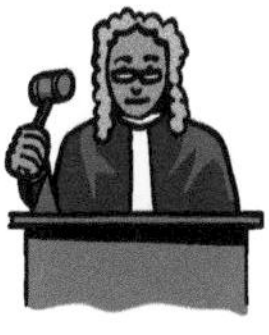

judge

judge

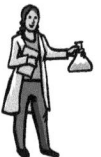

chemist

chemist

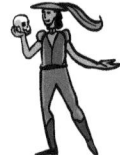

actor

actor

bus driver

bus driver

taxi driver

taxi driver

fisherman

fisherman

cleaning lady

cleaning lady

roofer

roofer

waiter

waiter

hunter

hunter

painter

painter

baker

baker

electrician

electrician

builder

builder

engineer

engineer

butcher

butcher

plumber

plumber

postman

postman

soldier

soldier

architect

architect

cashier

cashier

florist

florist

hairdresser

hairdresser

conductor

conductor

mechanic

mechanic

captain

captain

dentist

dentist

scientist

scientist

rabbi

rabbi

imam

imam

monk

monk

pastor

clergyman

tools
tools

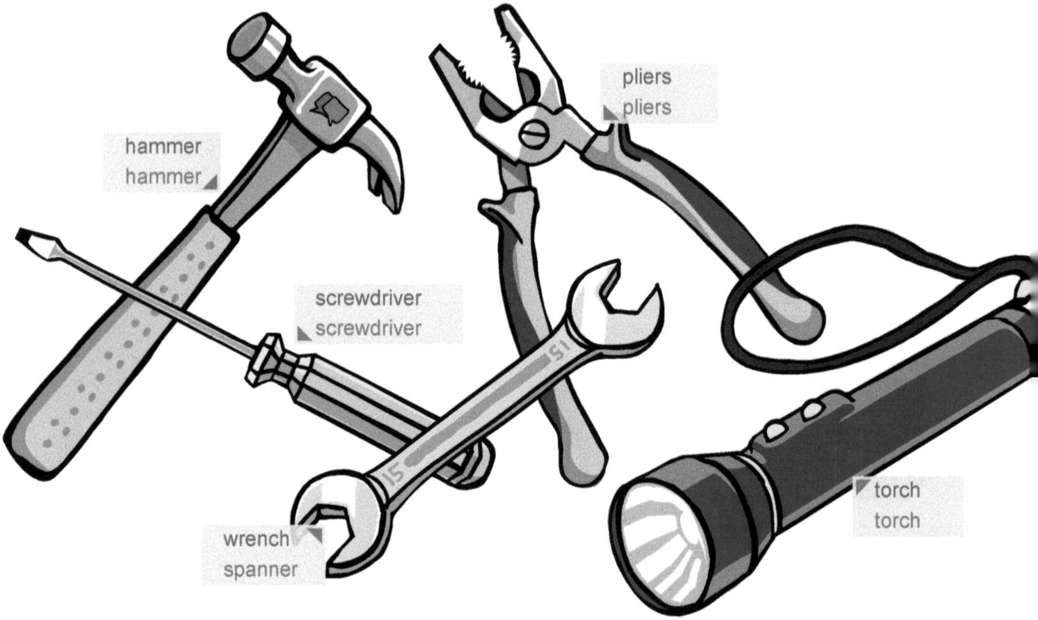
hammer
hammer
pliers
pliers
screwdriver
screwdriver
wrench
spanner
torch
torch

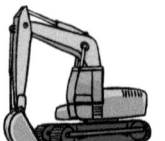

excavator

digger

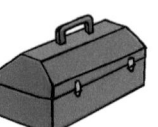

toolbox

toolbox

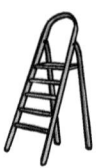

ladder

ladder

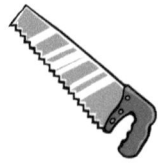

saw

saw

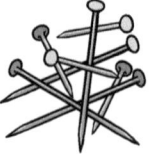

nails

nails

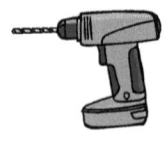

drill

drill

repair
repair

shovel
shovel

Damn!
Damn!

dustpan
dustpan

paint can
paint pot

screws
screws

musical instruments
musical instruments

drum set
drum kit

loud speaker
loudspeaker

guitar
guitar

double bass
double bass

trumpet
trumpet

piano

piano

violin

violin

bass

bass

timpani

timpani

drums

drums

keyboard

keyboard

saxophone

saxophone

flute

flute

microphone

microphone

ZOO

ZOO

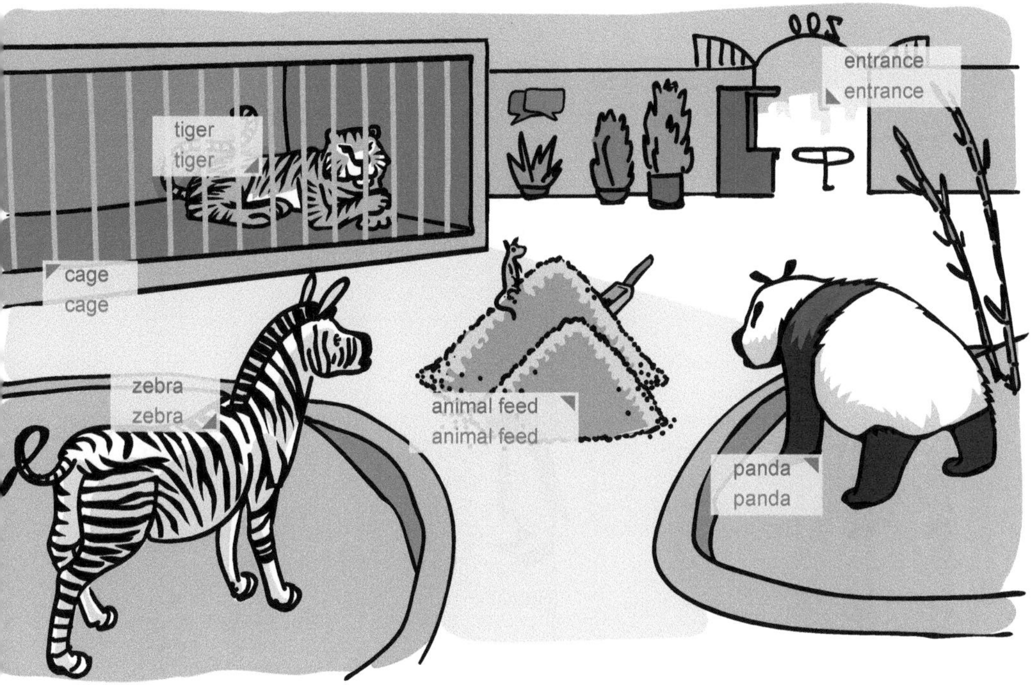

entrance
entrance
tiger
tiger
cage
cage
zebra
zebra
animal feed
animal feed
panda
panda

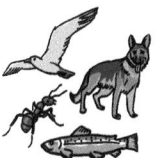

animals

animals

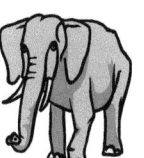

elephant

elephant

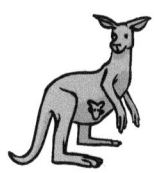

kangaroo

kangaroo

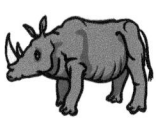

rhino

rhino

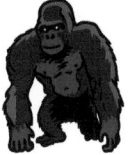

gorilla

gorilla

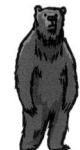

bear

bear

camel

camel

ostrich

ostrich

lion

lion

monkey

monkey

flamingo

flamingo

parrot

parrot

polar bear

polar bear

penguin

penguin

shark

shark

peacock

peacock

snake

snake

crocodile

crocodile

zookeeper

zookeeper

seal

seal

jaguar

jaguar

pony
pony

leopard
leopard

hippo
hippo

giraffe
giraffe

eagle
eagle

boar
boar

fish
fish

turtle
turtle

walrus
walrus

fox
fox

gazelle
gazelle

American football
American football

cycling
cycling

tennis
tennis

basketball
basketball

swimming
swimming

boxing
boxing

ice hockey
ice hockey

soccer	badminton	athletics
football	badminton	athletics

handball	skiing	polo
handball	skiing	polo

jump
jump

laugh
laugh

hug
hug

walk
walk

sing
sing

pray
pray

kiss
kiss

dream
dream

write
write

draw
draw

show
show

push
push

give
give

take
take

have
have

do
do

be
be

stand
stand

run
run

pull
pull

throw
throw

fall
fall

lie
lie

wait
wait

carry
carry

sit
sit

get dressed
get dressed

sleep
sleep

wake up
wake up

look at
look at

cry
cry

stroke
stroke

comb
comb

talk
talk

understand
understand

ask
ask

listen
listen

drink
drink

eat
eat

tidy up
tidy up

love
love

cook
cook

drive
drive

fly
fly

activities - activities

sail

sail

calculate

calculate

read

read

learn

learn

work

work

marry

marry

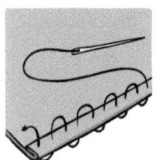

sew

sew

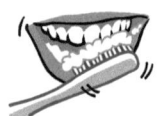

brush teeth

brush teeth

kill

kill

smoke

smoke

send

send

activities - activities

grandmother
grandmother

grandfather
grandfather

father
father

mother
mother

baby
baby

daughter
daughter

son
son

guest

guest

aunt

aunt

uncle

uncle

brother

brother

sister

sister

body
body

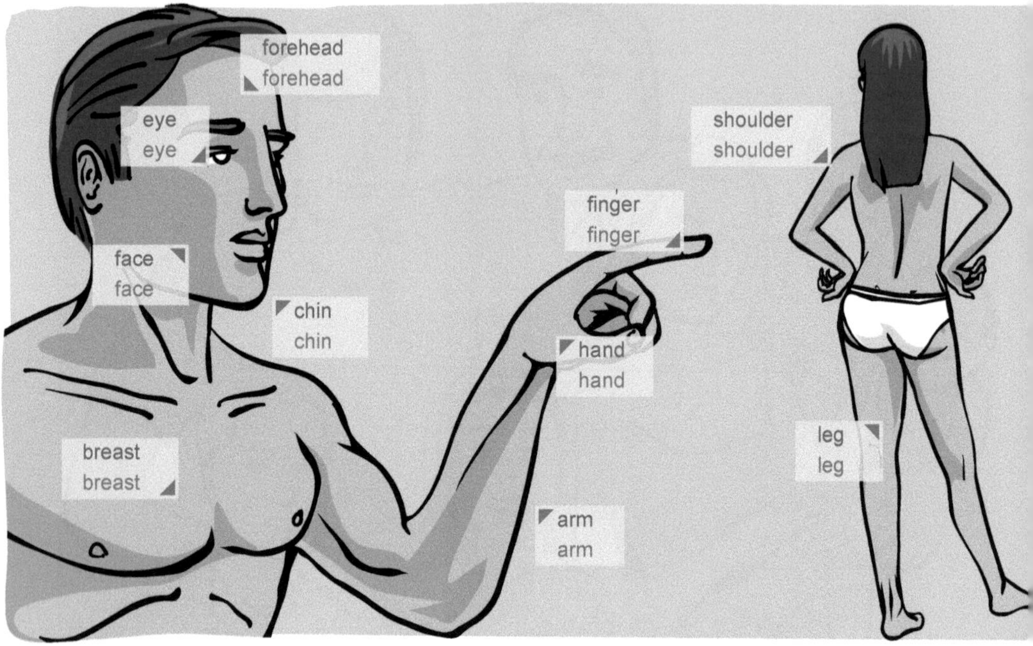

forehead
forehead

eye
eye

shoulder
shoulder

finger
finger

face
face

chin
chin

hand
hand

leg
leg

breast
breast

arm
arm

baby

baby

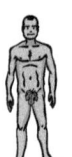

man

man

woman

woman

girl

girl

boy

boy

head

head

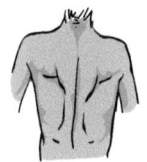

back
back

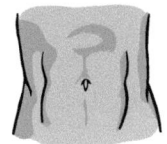

belly
belly

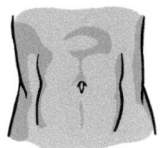

navel
belly button

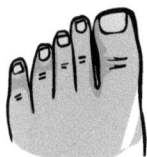

toe
toe

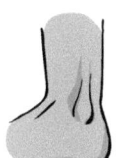

heel
heel

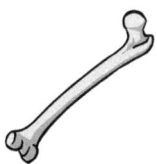

bone
bone

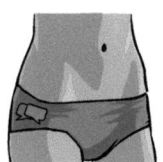

hip
hip

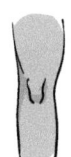

knee
knee

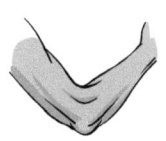

elbow
elbow

nose
nose

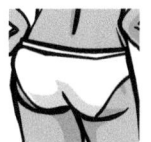

buttocks
bottom

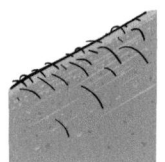

skin
skin

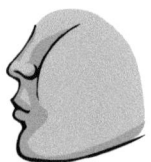

cheek
cheek

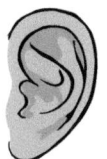

ear
ear

lip
lip

mouth

mouth

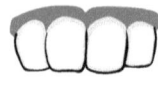

tooth

tooth

tongue

tongue

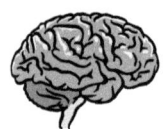

brain

brain

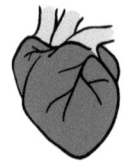

heart

heart

muscle

muscle

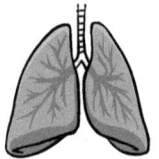

lung

lung

liver

liver

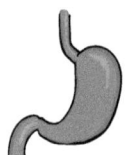

stomach

stomach

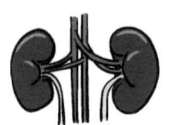

kidneys

kidneys

sex

sex

condom

condom

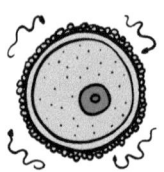

ovum

ovum

semen

semen

pregnancy

pregnancy

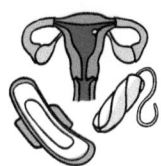

menstruation

menstruation

vagina

vagina

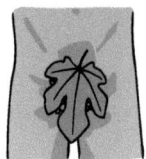

penis

penis

eyebrow

eyebrow

hair

hair

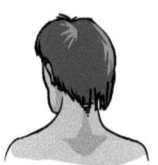

neck

neck

hospital

hospital

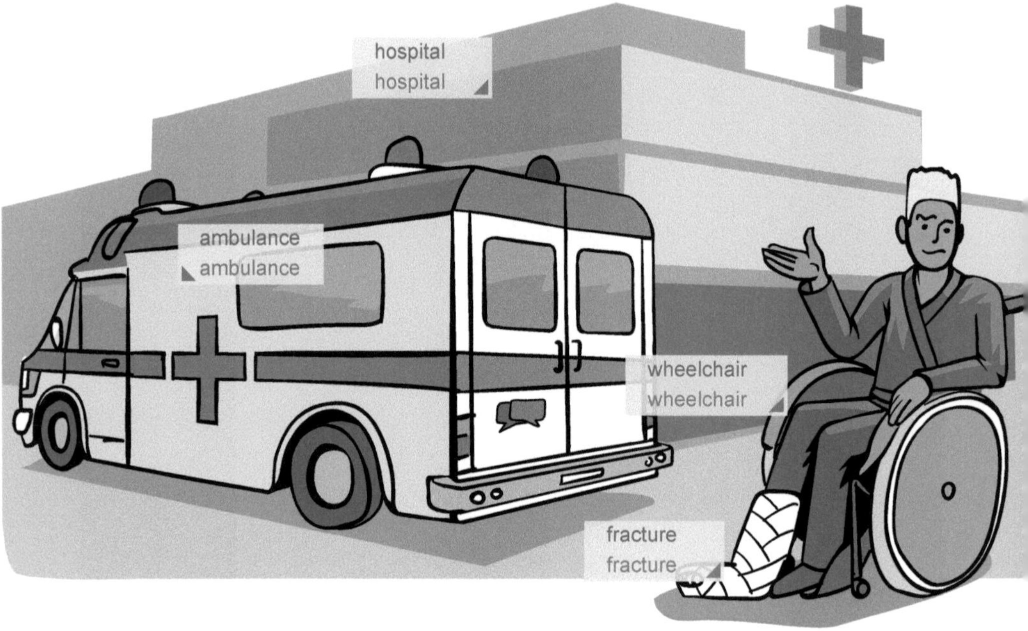

hospital
hospital
ambulance
ambulance
wheelchair
wheelchair
fracture
fracture

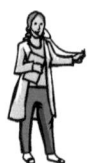

doctor

doctor

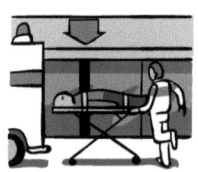

emergency room

emergency room

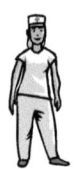

nurse

nurse

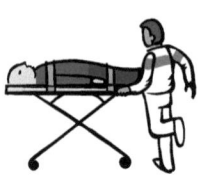

emergency

emergency

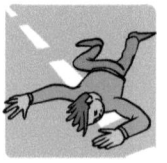

unconscious

unconscious

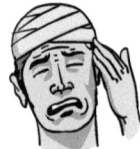

pain

pain

injury

injury

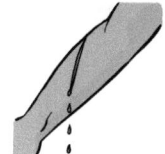

bleeding

bleeding

heart attack

heart attack

stroke

stroke

allergy

allergy

cough

cough

fever

fever

flu

flu

diarrhea

diarrhoea

headache

headache

cancer

cancer

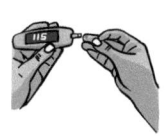

diabetes

diabetes

surgeon

surgeon

scalpel

scalpel

operation

operation

CT

CT

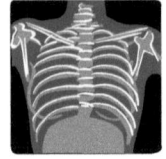

x-ray

x-ray

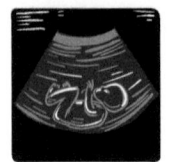

ultrasound

ultrasound

face mask

face mask

disease

disease

waiting room

waiting room

crutch

crutch

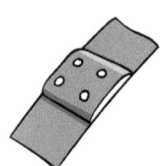

plaster

plaster

bandage

bandage

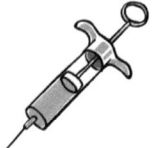

injection

injection

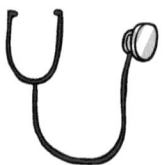

stethoscope

stethoscope

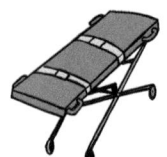

stretcher

stretcher

clinical thermometer

clinical thermometer

birth

birth

overweight

overweight

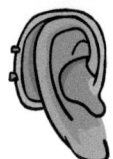

hearing aid

hearing aid

disinfectant

disinfectant

infection

infection

virus

virus

HIV / AIDS

HIV / AIDS

medicine

medicine

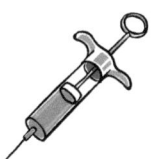

vaccination

vaccination

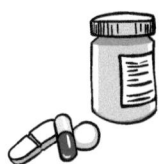

tablets

tablets

pill

pill

emergency call

emergency call

blood pressure monitor

blood pressure monitor

ill / healthy

ill / healthy

Help!

Help!

alarm

alarm

assault

assault

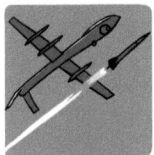

attack

attack

danger

danger

emergency exit

emergency exit

Fire!

Fire!

fire extinguisher

fire extinguisher

accident

accident

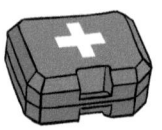

first-aid kit

first-aid kit

SOS

SOS

police

police

Europe

Europe

North America

North America

South America

South America

Africa

Africa

Asia

Asia

Australia

Australia

Atlantic

Atlantic

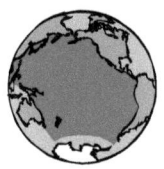

Pacific

Pacific

Indian Ocean

Indian Ocean

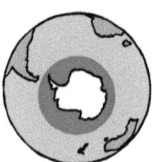

Antarctic Ocean

Antarctic Ocean

Arctic Ocean

Arctic Ocean

North pole

North Pole

South pole

South Pole

Antarctica

Antarctica

earth

Earth

land

land

sea

sea

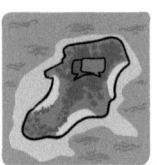

island

island

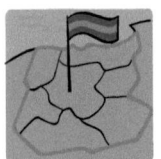

nation

nation

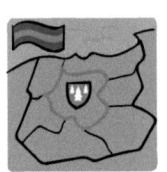

state

state

clock face

clock face

hour hand

hour hand

minute hand

minute hand

second hand

second hand

What time is it?

What time is it?

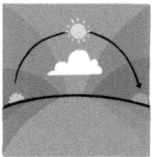

day

day

time

time

now

now

digital watch

digital watch

minute

minute

hour

hour

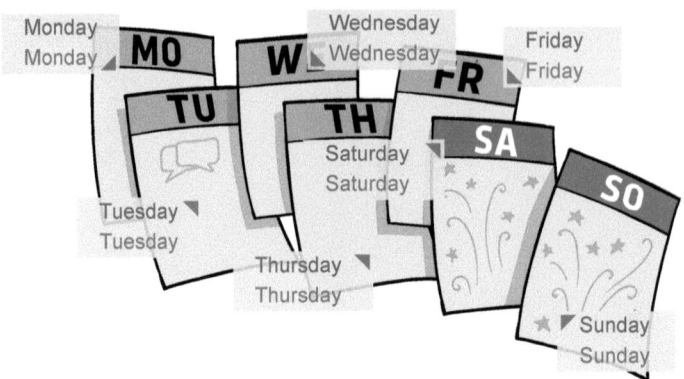

Monday
Monday
Tuesday
Tuesday
Wednesday
Wednesday
Thursday
Thursday
Friday
Friday
Saturday
Saturday
Sunday
Sunday

yesterday
....
yesterday

today
....
today

tomorrow
....
tomorrow

morning
....
morning

noon
....
noon

evening
....
evening

workdays
....
business days

weekend
....
weekend

year

year

rain
rain
spring
spring
summer
summer
wind
wind
fall
autumn
snow
snow
winter
winter

4.APRIL 11°
5.APRIL 4°
6.APRIL 13°
7.APRIL 8°
8.APRIL 10°

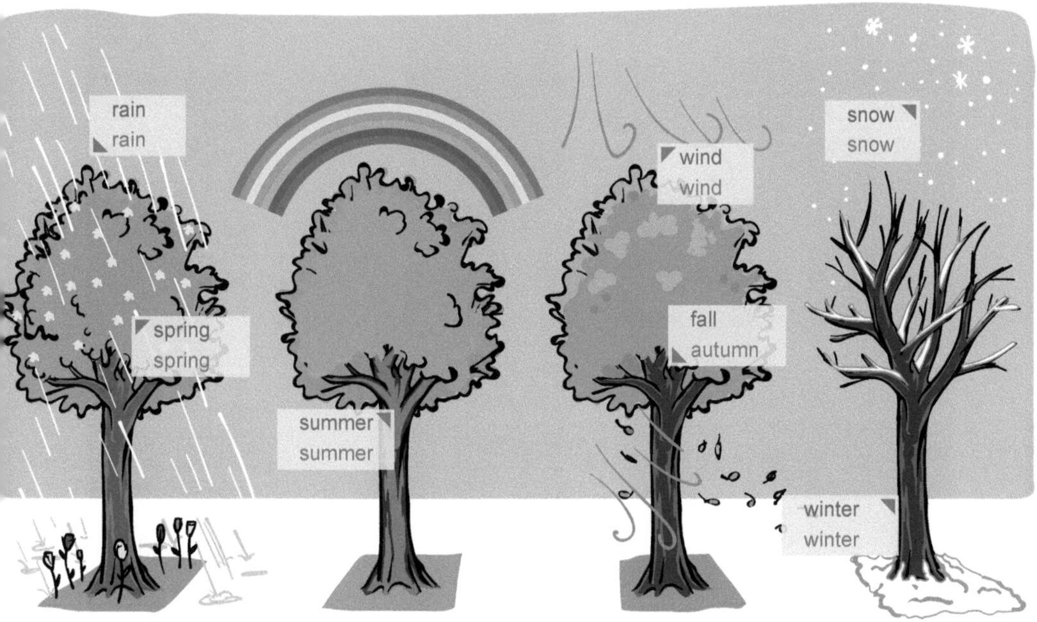

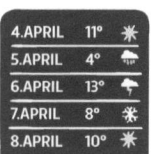

weather forecast

weather forecast

F C
120 40
90 30
60 20
30 10
0 0
-30 -10
-20

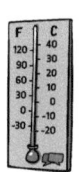

thermometer

thermometer

sunshine

sunshine

cloud

cloud

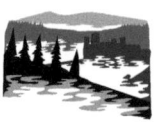

fog

fog

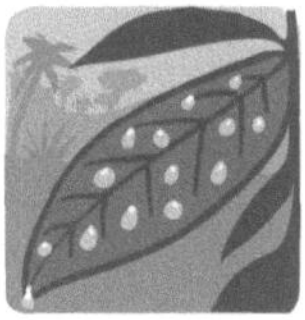

humidity

humidity

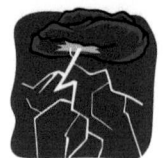

lightning

lightning

thunder

thunder

storm

storm

hail

hail

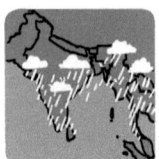

monsoon

monsoon

flood

flood

ice

ice

January

January

February

February

March

March

April

April

May

May

June

June

July

July

August

August

year - year

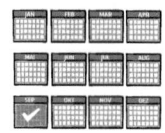

September
September

October
October

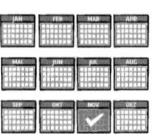

November
November

December
December

shapes
shapes

circle
circle

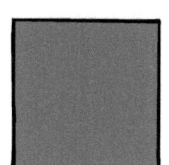

square
square

rectangle
rectangle

triangle
triangle

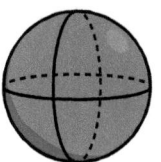

sphere
sphere

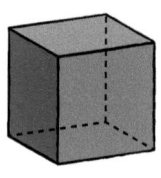

cube
cube

colors
colours

white

white

yellow

yellow

orange

orange

pink

pink

red

red

purple

purple

blue

blue

green

green

brown

brown

gray

grey

black

black

a lot / a little

a lot / a little

angry / calm

angry / calm

beautiful / ugly

beautiful / ugly

beginning / end

beginning / end

big / small

big / small

bright / dark

bright / dark

brother / sister

brother / sister

clean / dirty

clean / dirty

complete / incomplete

complete / incomplete

day / night

day / night

dead / alive

dead / alive

wide / narrow

wide / narrow

edible / inedible

edible / inedible

evil / kind

evil / kind

excited / bored

excited / bored

fat / thin

fat / thin

first / last

first / last

friend / enemy

friend / enemy

full / empty

full / empty

hard / soft

hard / soft

heavy / light

heavy / light

hunger / thirst

hunger / thirst

ill / healthy

ill / healthy

illegal / legal

illegal / legal

intelligent / stupid

intelligent / stupid

left / right

left / right

near / far

near / far

new / used
new / used

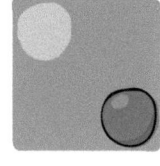

nothing / something
nothing / something

old / young
old / young

on / off
on / off

open / closed
open / closed

quiet / loud
quiet / loud

rich / poor
rich / poor

right / wrong
right / wrong

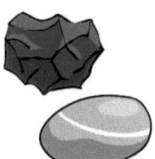

rough / smooth
rough / smooth

sad / happy
sad / happy

short / long
short / long

slow / fast
slow / fast

wet / dry
wet / dry

warm / cool
warm / cool

war / peace
war / peace

0

zero

zero

1

one

one

2

two

two

3

three

three

4

four

four

5

five

five

6

six

six

7

seven

seven

8

eight

eight

9

nine

nine

10

ten

ten

11

eleven

eleven

12
twelve

twelve

13
thirteen

thirteen

14
fourteen

fourteen

15
fifteen

fifteen

16
sixteen

sixteen

17
seventeen

seventeen

18
eighteen

eighteen

19
nineteen

nineteen

20
twenty

twenty

100
hundred

hundred

1.000
thousand

thousand

1.000.000
million

million

English

English

American English

American English

Chinese Mandarin

Chinese Mandarin

Hindi

Hindi

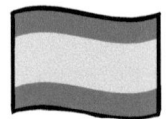

Spanish

Spanish

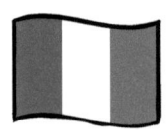

French

French

Arabic

Arabic

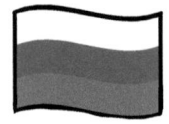

Russian

Russian

Portuguese

Portuguese

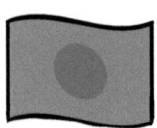

Bengali

Bengali

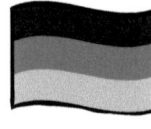

German

German

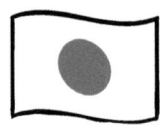

Japanese

Japanese

I
I

you
you

he / she / it
he / she / it

we
we

you
you

they
they

who?
who?

what?
what?

how?
how?

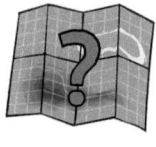

where?
where?

when?
when?

name
name

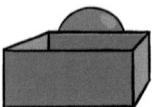

behind
behind

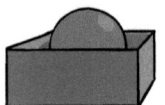

in
in

in front of
in front of

over
over

on
on

under
under

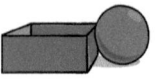

beside
beside

between
between

place
place